P9-DID-755

CHRISTOPHER PAOLINI

CHRISTOPHER PAOLINI

LISA WADE MCCORMICK

ROSEN
PUBLISHING®

New York

*To the sources of magic in my life: Dave, Wade, Maddie,
Shadow, Kona, Paula, Carl, and Lynda*

Published in 2013 by The Rosen Publishing Group, Inc.
29 East 21st Street, New York, NY 10010

First Edition

Library of Congress Cataloging-in-Publication Data

McCormick, Lisa Wade, 1961–
Christopher Paolini/Lisa Wade McCormick.—1st ed.
    p. cm.—(All about the author)
Includes bibliographical references and index.
ISBN 978-1-4488-6939-8 (library binding)
1. Paolini, Christopher—Juvenile literature. 2. Fantasy
fiction—Authorship—Juvenile literature. 3. Authors,
American—21st century—Biography—Juvenile literature.
I. Title.
PS3616.A55Z77 2013
813'.6—dc23
[B]
                                                    2011043296

Manufactured in the United States of America

CPSIA Compliance Information: Batch #S12YA: For further information, contact Rosen Publishing, New York,
New York, at 1-800-237-9932.

CONTENTS

Author Christopher Paolini has cast a spell on millions of readers with his magical books about a boy named Eragon and his beautiful dragon, Saphira. Paolini's writing isn't the only thing in his world touched by magic. Some of that mystic power seems to have seeped off the page and into his personal life. How else could a teenager from Montana become one of the most celebrated children's book authors in the world?

The magical moment that changed Paolini's life happened in an Albertsons grocery store in Livingston, Montana. During the summer of 2002, the wife of author Carl Hiaasen stopped at the store and stumbled upon a copy of Paolini's self-published book, *Eragon*. She bought it for her twelve-year-old son, Ryan. The story captured Ryan's imagination. He couldn't stop reading the dragon tale that Paolini wrote when he was just fifteen.

"We didn't hear from him for hours," Hiaasen, author of such children's books as *Hoot* and *Flush*, said in an interview on *The Artist's Craft*, a television show on the Raleigh Television Network. "I think he finished it the next day."

When Ryan described the book as "better than Harry Potter," the famous series about a young wizard, Hiaasen called his publisher. "I said there's

Christopher Paolini often dreamed about dragons when he was a boy. Those dreams inspired him to write his first fantasy novel, *Eragon*, at the age of fifteen.

this kid [and] I think you ought to take a look at this book he's published," Hiaasen said. A short time later, New York publisher Alfred A. Knopf, a division of Random House, signed a three-book deal with Paolini. The teenager's writing career took flight. It soared faster than his imaginary dragon.

Paolini's first book, *Eragon*, arrived in bookstores in August 2003. The sweeping fantasy, filled with dragons, elves, and an evil ruler, sold millions of copies around the world. The nineteen-year-old writer became an international sensation.

Hiaasen downplayed his role in discovering the young dragon writer. "The truth is, he's a talented kid, and he would have been discovered and this would have happened to him eventually, I'm sure," Hiaasen said in his interview with *The Artist's Craft*.

Paolini continued to charm readers with his stories about the bond between Eragon and Saphira. His second book, *Eldest*, was released on August 23, 2005. The best-selling novel sold more than 425,000 copies in its first week.

Fox 2000 Pictures later released a major motion picture based on Paolini's stories. The movie *Eragon* opened in theaters nationwide in December 2006.

Back in Montana, Paolini started working on the third book in his series. *Brisingr* arrived in bookstores on September 20, 2008. It sold a record 550,000 copies the first day.

The adventures of Eragon and Saphira weren't over yet. As Paolini wrote the 748-page *Brisingr*, he discovered he needed more words to finish his epic fantasy. His trilogy became a four-book series, known as the Inheritance Cycle. The magical series concludes with the title *Inheritance*. Knopf released the much-anticipated novel on November 8, 2011. Before *Inheritance* went on sale, Paolini promised fans that the answers to all their burning questions would be revealed in the final book.

In this book, many answers to readers' burning questions about Christopher Paolini will also be revealed. His personal story doesn't have any epic battles or wicked kings, but it is filled with heroes, dreams, and of course, magic.

ONE

LIFE BEFORE DRAGONS

In the days before dragons, elves, and heroic battles ruled Christopher Paolini's world, the young author led a simple and sheltered life. He came from humble beginnings and never imagined he would become an international publishing phenomenon.

A RUSTIC LIFESTYLE

The author's mother, Talita, was a Montessori schoolteacher. His father, Kenneth, worked as a photographer and later started a small publishing company. Christopher, their first child, was born on November 17, 1983, in Southern California. The family later moved to Alaska. According to an article by Cecelia Goodnow of the *Seattle Post-Intelligencer*, Christopher and his family lived in a small, leaky log cabin in

Anchorage. "I remember us having to use chewing gum to plug up the gaps," he told Goodnow.

In 1991, the family moved to Paradise Valley, Montana. The future writer spent much of his boyhood in a farmhouse on the banks of the Yellowstone River. A story in the *Telegraph*, a newspaper based in the United Kingdom, described the home as a "cramped living room with an old sofa and a wood-burning stove, a kitchen with a bare linoleum floor, a dark study, and a few bedrooms."

Christopher, however, still enjoyed a rich and charmed childhood. He spent his days hiking in snowcapped mountains, swimming in the river, and making bows and arrows with his younger sister, Angela.

PARENTS AS TEACHERS

Christopher and his sister were homeschooled by their parents. The couple didn't think a traditional school would be a good fit for their children, who could read by the time they were three. According to Montanakids.com, Christopher tested "off the charts" for kindergarten. His parents worried a regular kindergarten class wouldn't challenge their son. They had concerns about letting him skip grades, too.

In an interview with the *New York Times*, Kenneth Paolini also said he wanted his children to have time "to watch the clouds, to have thinking spaces."

Christopher Paolini grew up in a small house along the banks of the Yellowstone River near Paradise Valley, Montana. He and his younger sister, Angela, were homeschooled by their parents.

Christopher's mother tailored classroom lessons to her children's passions. When Christopher showed an interest in pirates, for example, she let him make a pirate map for an assignment. "And [I] soaked it in tea and singed the edges so it looked like a real pirate map," he told the *New York Times*.

His parents made books and reading a key part of their children's education. The couple started reading to the children as infants. "Reading was a pleasurable time when they felt loved, secure, and supremely happy," Talita Paolini wrote in *Home Education Magazine*.

Christopher read his first word when he was a toddler, his mother said. The word wasn't "dragon," though. It was another four-legged animal. "He got a faraway look in his eyes,

At one point early in his life, Christopher Paolini didn't like to read. That changed when his mother took him to the library and he discovered books that sparked his imagination.

then he repeated the word 'c-a-t,'" Talita recalled in *Home Education Magazine*. "He looked at me with a twinkle in his eye and a smile that grew wider and wider. 'Cat,' he said. 'CAT!' He leaped up and ran to get a picture of a cat. He could read."

At one point in his life, however, the young author didn't like to read. It happened when he was four. "I remember marching up to my mom and telling her I hate to read and didn't see how it had any use in the real world," Paolini told the *Missoulian*. "Fortunately, she didn't listen to me." His mother didn't give up on him, either. She worked with him until the letters and words started to make sense. Then she took him to the library.

By Walter Crane

Christopher Paolini is a fan of books and artworks about dragons, like this illustration by nineteenth-century English artist Walter Crane. This is Crane's *Prince Cheri and the Dragon* (1878).

DISCOVERING NEW WORLDS

"That single event changed my life," Paolini wrote
in an essay on BookBrowse.com. "In the library, hidden in the children's section, was a series of short
mystery novels." His eyes zeroed in on a book with
a bright cover. He flipped through the pages. The
words came to life. A story in which tomato sauce
was mistaken for blood triggered his imagination.
"I discovered another world, peopled with interesting characters facing compelling situations," Paolini
wrote in his essay. "From then on, I've been in love
with the written word."

Paolini said he's read more than three thousand
books. As a boy, he checked out stacks of books
from his local library. "I was picking up six, seven,
eight books at a time and going back the next week
to pick up another pile of books," Paolini said in an
interview with *Wyoming Library Roundup* magazine.

Those weekly trips to the library are still etched
in Talita Paolini's mind. "I can still see my son struggling to navigate down the front steps of the library
with a stack of books in his arms nearly over his
head, his sister similarly laden at his side," she wrote
in *Home Education Magazine*.

Christopher read everything from classics to
mysteries. But he always came back to fantasy novels and stories about dragons, dwarfs, and damsels

INSPIRATION FOR ALAGAËSIA

The stories in Christopher Paolini's Inheritance Cycle are set in a magical land called Alagaësia. Parts of this mysterious world are covered with dense forests and the jagged Beor Mountains. Other parts are bleak and hostile. There's even a creepy area called the Spine, which runs up and down the eastern border of Alagaësia. "Strange tales and men often come from those mountains, usually boding ill," Paolini wrote of the Spine in his book *Eragon*.

Mystical people and beasts also live in the imaginary land of Alagaësia, which Paolini created as the backdrop for his epic fantasy novels. There are elves, dwarves, shape-shifting "werecats," and horn-headed monsters called Urgals.

Paolini said the inspiration for Alagaësia came right outside his front door. The best-selling author grew up along the Yellowstone River in Paradise Valley, Montana. His home is nestled among the rugged Absaroka, Gallatin, and Beartooth mountain ranges. "We have the most incredible landscape where we live," Paolini said in an interview with *Boys' Life* magazine. "That has always inspired me."

Paolini spent his childhood hiking in nearby pine forests. He camped in the snowcapped mountains, where grizzly bears, wolves, moose, and antelope still roam free. He told *Boys' Life*, "I think when you have that much time by yourself and you're...out in the wild, you start making up stories to tell yourself and making up stories about your surroundings."

In an interview with *Distinctly Montana*, Paolini talked about the inspirational role the Beartooth Mountains played in his book *Eragon*. "The 'ten-mile-high' mountains in Eragon are a tribute to them," he said. "Some days when I look at their snow-capped peaks, I can almost see the dragon Saphira soaring over them, her brilliant sapphire-blue scales reflecting the sun and snow."

Paolini said he has no plans to leave Montana or the beauty that inspired his popular children's books. "I can't think of a better place to live," he said in an interview with *Wyoming Library Roundup*. "I grew up here. My family is here. The landscape is beautiful and the people are friendly and wonderful. I can't imagine being happy living in the middle of the city."

in distress. He told Teenreads.com, "I enjoy fantasy because it allows me to visit lands that have never existed, to see things that never could exist, to experience daring adventures with interesting characters, and most importantly, to feel the sense of magic in the world."

THE DRAGON WRITER'S KEYS TO SUCCESS

Paolini said reading helped him become a successful writer. But his parents and their decision to educate him at home played even bigger roles. "Everything I did was only possible because my parents were dedicated and loving enough to homeschool my sister and me," Paolini wrote in an essay on BookBrowse.com.

In an interview with Rebecca Kochenderfer of Homeschool.com, Paolini said his educational background gave him opportunities that he might not have received in a traditional classroom setting. "One of the biggest advantages of being homeschooled was being able to concentrate on the subjects that I was interested in," he said.

Paolini, for example, had the chance to develop his artistic skills. His artwork appears in some of his books, including a map he sketched of the mystical land of Alagaësia. Paolini drew the blue dragon that appears on the cover of the self-published version of *Eragon*.

The towering Absaroka Mountain Range near Paolini's Montana home inspired the mystical land of Alagaësia that he created for his books.

There's also an illustration he inked of the evil King Galbatorix in *Brisingr*.

A HIGH SCHOOL DIPLOMA AT FIFTEEN

When Christopher and his sister were ready for high school, his parents stopped teaching them. They enrolled their children in the American School, an accredited distance-learning program in Lansing, Illinois. Christopher took online classes to earn his high school diploma. He graduated at the age of fifteen.

Christopher planned to go to college and received a full scholarship to Reed College in Portland, Oregon. "I literally had the orientation papers on my desk," he told the *Christian Science Monitor*. His father, however, wasn't sold on the idea. Kenneth Paolini thought his son was too young to go to college.

The budding author had to plot another course for his next chapter in life. He told *USA TODAY*, "I didn't have a job, and the nearest town was some twenty miles [32 kilometers] away. I needed a way of entertaining myself." He started writing. At first, it was a hobby. "I was completely bored," Paolini told the *Missoulian*. "I had nothing to do. And I absolutely love stories."

Writing, however, soon became a personal challenge. "I decided to try and write something I would enjoy reading," Paolini said in an interview with the *New York Times*. He envisioned a story filled with magic, fire-breathing dragons, hideous creatures, bloody battles, beautiful maidens, and, of course, a hero.

Paolini drew inspiration from the science fiction and fantasy novels he had read as a child. Some of his favorite books included *Magician* by Raymond E. Feist and the *Lord of the Rings* trilogy by J. R. R. Tolkien. One book, however, struck a deeper chord with Paolini. It's the book that planted the seed for what is now his number one best-selling novel, *Eragon*. "When I was about 12 or 13 I read a book called *Jeremy Thatcher, Dragon Hatcher* [by Bruce Coville]," Paolini told *Time For Kids*. "It is about a young boy who went into a mysterious shop and bought a dragon egg that ends up hatching. It stuck in my head. *Eragon* was an attempt to see what I could do with [the idea] myself."

During an interview with CNN, Paolini discussed how Coville's book shaped his best-selling novel. "I loved that idea so much of a young boy finding a dragon egg that I asked myself three questions. I said, What land would a dragon come from? Who would find the dragon egg out in the middle of nowhere, and since dragon eggs can't be that common, who else would be looking for a dragon?"

The fifteen-year-old was now ready to start his writing quest. His path would take him through the imaginary land of Alagaësia. Along the way, he would befriend a farm boy named Eragon, soar on the back of a blue dragon named Saphira, seek revenge against an evil king and his dark forces, and even rescue a princess.

Christopher Paolini took the first step in his mystical journey when he penned thirteen haunting words: "Wind howled through the night, carrying a scent that would change the world."

A DRAGON IS BORN

Author Christopher Paolini once told a group of students that words have the power to change the world. He should know. The words he penned as a teenager transformed the once-unknown writer into a best-selling children's book author.

When Paolini started writing a fantasy about the magical bond between a farm boy and his blue dragon, he didn't know where his words would take him. "I was only fifteen when I started *Eragon*," Paolini told the *Telegraph*. "I didn't know how to write. I just told everything in one gigantic burst."

Images that had swirled in his mind for years poured out on paper. He envisioned a boy sailing on a dragon's back. He saw

Before he wrote *Eragon*, Paolini studied the epic poem *Beowulf*. Grendel is the horned monster that is killed by Beowulf, a Scandinavian warrior.

the two embark on a quest for revenge to a mystical land filled with elves, dwarves, bloody battles, beautiful maidens, an evil ruler, and dark magic. "The first draft came so easily, it was like a dam had broken," Paolini said in an interview with the *New York Times*.

TEEN AUTHOR

The homeschooled author from Paradise Valley, Montana, spent hours on a faded couch in his family's living room writing the epic fantasy. The young prodigy had already graduated from high school and had a lot of time on his hands. "I didn't have too many activities aside from the ones I invented," he told the *New York Times*. "A lot of writing is about getting the time and space."

Paolini divided his time between writing and research. He read books on the craft of writing. He studied the books, poems, myths, and medieval tales that inspired him as a boy. He looked for patterns and themes in his favorite works, including J. R. R. Tolkien's *Lord of the Rings* and the Old English epic poem *Beowulf*.

"The challenge was that he was learning to write professionally while working on a novel-length manuscript," Paolini's mother, Talita, wrote in *Home Education Magazine*.

Paolini is extremely close to his younger sister, Angela. A feisty witch and herbalis character in his books is based on and named after her.

A THREE-YEAR WRITING JOURNEY

It took Christopher Paolini a year to finish the first draft of his 200,000-word novel, *Eragon*. The sixteen-year-old writer wasn't satisfied with the results, though. It wasn't the story he set out to write. It wasn't a story that he would want to read—not yet, anyway.

He spent a second year revising his book. He wrote for hours every day. "He tackled each paragraph with zeal, trying to convey the drama that played out in his mind," his mother wrote in *Home Education Magazine*.

When he finished the second version of his manuscript, he showed it to his parents. "Once we were given the second draft of the book, we saw that there was something very special there," his father, Kenneth, told the *Missoulian*.

GUINNESS WORLD RECORD HOLDER

Christopher Paolini is not only an internationally best-selling children's book author, he's also an official world-record holder. During the 2011 BookExpo America (BEA), Guinness World Records officially recognized the Montana writer as the Youngest Author of a Best-Selling Book Series.

Paolini wrote the first draft of his fantasy novel, *Eragon*, at the age of fifteen. Over the next decade, Paolini wrote three more best-selling novels in his acclaimed fantasy series, known as the Inheritance Cycle: *Eldest*, *Brisingr*, and *Inheritance*. Paolini's books have climbed to the top of the *New York Times* and other best-seller lists. More than twenty-five million copies have been sold around the world. Guinness World Records defines a best-selling series as one that sells more than twenty million copies.

"While younger authors have been published, no one else has achieved anything approaching the phenomenal success [of] Christopher's work," said Stuart Claxton, spokesman for Guinness World Records. "While most kids were outside playing, Christopher was crafting a work of impressive scope and imagination that will forever live on the page."

Paolini said he read the *Guinness World Records* books as a boy but never imagined he would be included in one. He is featured in *Guinness World Records 2012*, which hit bookstores in September 2011.

The novel became a family project. Christopher's parents and his younger sister, Angela, took on roles as editors. Kenneth and Talita Paolini were authors themselves. They coauthored a nonfiction book about the lessons Christopher's mother learned as a Montessori schoolteacher. That book is titled *Play and Learn with Cereal O's: Simple, Effective Activities to Help You Educate Your Preschool Child*. The couple also collaborated on a book called *400 Years of Imaginary Friends*, which takes a close and critical look at religious cults.

Christopher and his family spent a third year editing *Eragon*, the first installment in the four-book Inheritance Cycle. "My parents didn't suggest changes in the plot line," Paolini told the *New York Times*. They did, however, fix his grammar, move sentences around, and work on the story's flow and continuity. "I learned so much," Paolini told the newspaper.

DECISION TO SELF-PUBLISH

In 2001, Paolini and his family took a chance with *Eragon*. They published the book through their own small publishing company, Paolini International, LLC. "My family and I chose to self-publish *Eragon* because we wanted to retain financial and creative control over the book," Paolini said in an interview with Teenreads.com. "Also, we were excited by the prospect of working on this project as a family."

Paolini drew the dragon eye that appeared on the book's cover. He also sketched a map of the book's setting, the mystical land Alagaësia. Paolini's mother and sister proofread the book. His father typeset the manuscript. Using the family's savings, the Paolinis paid a printer to produce several thousand copies, and they made plans to go out into the world to sell them. The first copies of *Eragon* rolled off the presses in November 2001. The book sold for $22.95 in retail stores. The family charged students $14.00.

TAKING HIS STORY ON THE ROAD

For the next year, the teenage author traveled across the country marketing his 472-page paperback novel. "'We went to places that never had an author, places hungry for this," Paolini said in a *New York Times* interview. The first-time novelist did readings and signings in bookstores. He autographed all his books with the same tagline: "May your swords stay sharp!" It's a phrase he borrowed from *Eragon*.

In schools and libraries, Paolini gave a presentation called "Why Read? Why Write?" He dressed like a medieval storyteller for those visits. He wore a red shirt with billowy sleeves, black pants, lace-up black leather boots, and a black beret. "It was intense," he told *Boys' Life*. "I dare anyone to put on a medieval costume when you're seventeen and walk into a strange high school. It was a great experience, but definitely a formative experience."

Paolini visited more than 135 schools and libraries across the country to promote *Eragon*. The young writer always took time to answer students' questions, like the ones he once fielded from a group of third and fourth graders in Montana. "How many words are in your book?" one boy asked. "About 200,000," Paolini answered. "How old is Eragon?" another student asked. "He's fifteen at the beginning of the book and sixteen by the end," Paolini said. A third student raised her hand and asked, "What is the meaning of life?"

According to the *Missoulian*, Paolini gave the inquisitive girl an honest and simple answer: "The closest I can come is to say to be as happy as you can be and make others as happy as you can."

Paolini did his best to honor those words. He went to extraordinary lengths to make his audiences happy and get them interested in his book. "I'm particularly fond of the time when I arm-wrestled a young man to get him to read *Eragon*," he told Teenreads.com. "Fortunately I won."

After nearly a year, though, life on the road started to take its toll on Paolini and his family. "Selling the book meant putting food on the table," Paolini told a reporter with the *Observer* newspaper in the United Kingdom. If the book did not start to turn a profit, the Paolinis would have had to find regular jobs to make ends meet.

BIG BREAK

Fate, however, intervened. In a scene ripped from the pages of a fantasy novel, a hero showed up just in time to save the struggling young author and his family.

The hero turned out to be a twelve-year-old boy named Ryan. He read *Eragon* during a fly-fishing trip to Montana in the summer of 2002, and he told his stepfather that it was better than Harry Potter. Ryan's stepfather, novelist Carl Hiaasen, told his publisher about the teenage writer and his dragon-inspired tale. The company soon signed a three-book contract with Paolini, which the *New York Times* said was worth an amount in "the middle six figures."

Paolini remembers the exact moment he learned that publisher Alfred A. Knopf (a division of Random House) was interested in his book. He was promoting *Eragon* at the Northwest Bookfest in Seattle,

Best-selling author Carl Hiaasen is credited with discovering Christopher Paolini in 2002. After his stepson read Paolini's self-published version of *Eragon*, Hiaasen old his publisher about the talented young author.

Washington, when he received an e-mail from his future editor, Michelle Frey. "My first reaction was one of disbelief, since I had no idea how Michelle could have heard about *Eragon*," Paolini told Teenreads.com. "This was quickly followed by cautious optimism; after all, I had no idea what terms Knopf was willing to offer. Once I did, my family and I were screaming with excitement."

Paolini and his family continue to express their appreciation for Hiaasen. "He changed our lives forever," Paolini told the *Telegraph*. "It made all the difference to get the support of someone like that."

Knopf released its version of *Eragon* on August 26, 2003. Editor Michelle Frey cut twenty thousand words from Paolini's original version of the book. She kept his story line in place, though. *Eragon* became an overnight publishing sensation. *U.S. News and World Report* hailed Paolini's debut novel as the "it" book in children's literature. A former editor at *Newsweek* said the teen writer wielded a pen that was "as mighty as his sword."

Eragon flew off bookstore shelves faster than the brilliant blue dragon, Saphira, could soar. It zoomed to the top of the *New York Times* best-seller lists. And Paolini's rise in the publishing world—and in fans' hearts—was far from over. Paolini's success gave credence to the words he once shared with a group of students in Corvallis, Montana. "I read because words have the power to change the world," the *Missoulian* quoted him as saying. "I write for the same reasons. I write to share adventures with people."

Paolini's own adventure was just starting. His hero, Eragon, and the beautiful dragon, Saphira, would face many more dangers and daring battles in their quest to save the empire.

THREE

CHAPTER

THE DRAGON WRITER SOARS

In the fall of 2003, a magical chapter unfolded in Christopher Paolini's young life. The struggling author's words turned to gold on an August day in 2003 when publisher Alfred A. Knopf released *Eragon*, the nineteen-year-old's five-hundred-page fantasy novel.

The company printed one hundred thousand hardcover copies of the mythical story about a farm boy named Eragon and his telepathic bond with a blue dragon named Saphira. "Her relationship with Eragon is really the heart of the story," Paolini said in an interview with Bill Thompson of *Eye on Books*. "It's a very profound bond."

News of the epic fantasy written by an unknown teen author spread quickly in the publishing world. Paolini's backstory as a homeschooled writer who inked the first draft of Eragon at age fifteen fueled interest in the book.

ERAGON TAKES FLIGHT

Eragon debuted at number three on the *New York Times* best-seller list for children's chapter books. "Most of the authors on that list aren't first-time authors," Paolini told the *Missoulian*. "It was definitely a huge surprise."

Publisher Alfred A. Knopf released *Eragon* in August 2003. The five-hundred-page fantasy about a farm boy's telepathic bond with his blue dragon, Saphira, became an instant best seller around the world.

By October 2003, 250,000 copies of *Eragon* were in print. The book had risen to the forty-first spot on *USA TODAY*'s top 150 best-selling books list. During the same time, Paolini launched a nationwide book tour for his breakout novel. He also traveled to the United Kingdom.

The best-selling author, however, no longer wore his medieval costume when he talked about his book. "It would take an act of God to get me back in that costume," Paolini told *USA TODAY*. "I don't need to fight for attention anymore."

Knopf made sure Paolini and his book received plenty of publicity. According to *Distinctly Montana* magazine, the publisher budgeted $500,000 to promote *Eragon*. The campaign included a book tour, cards, direct flyers, and ads in such publications as the *New York Times*, *USA TODAY*, and *Rolling Stone*. Paolini also appeared on the *Late Show with David Letterman* and the *Today Show*. "It's an exciting, new experience, totally different from anything I've done before," Paolini wrote in an essay on BookBrowse.com.

THE 21ST-CENTURY TOLKIEN

Eragon kept rising on the literary charts. By December 2003, the book had captured the number one position on the *New York Times* best-seller list for children's chapter books. It knocked off the acclaimed *Harry Potter and the Order of the Phoenix* to grab the top spot. Paolini, a dark-haired boy with glasses who resembled J. K. Rowling's young wizard, became known as the "Hotter Potter." The *Telegraph* came up with another nickname for Paolini. One of its headlines called him the "21st-Century Tolkien," a reference to the *Lord of the Rings* author.

Over the next two months, *Eragon* continued to make literary magic. In February 2004, just six months after the book was released, Knopf announced that one million copies of *Eragon* were in print. The book had held its number one position on the *New York Times* best-seller list for twenty-six consecutive weeks. It was among the top books on the *Book Sense* and *Publishers Weekly* best-seller lists, too. Overseas, *Eragon* had become the most popular children's book in the United Kingdom, Ireland, and Australia.

Paolini was now worth millions. He no longer had to worry about whether he could support his family. "The biggest change is simply our security…not having to worry about things as much," Paolini told the *Missoulian*.

STAYING GROUNDED

He and his family, however, maintained their humble lifestyle in rural Montana. They didn't move out of their small farmhouse along the Yellowstone River.

The popularity of Paolini's book *Eragon* made the first-time author a millionaire when he was only nineteen.

They continued shopping at a local Costco, a wholesale warehouse store. They saved their new-found fortune. "It's our main stream of income," Paolini's younger sister, Angela, told the *Telegraph*. "We have to be careful how we spend it."

The family did splurge on a few items, though. "My dad bought a new computer, and we got this really cool plasma-screen TV," Paolini said in an interview with the *Telegraph*. "The picture is so good, we don't go to the movies anymore. We just stay home and watch DVDs." According to Paolini, the family has more than four thousand movies in their collection. As a boy, he and his family watched a movie almost every night.

Paolini made one extravagant purchase, too. He bought a replica of a Viking sword. "I carry it every-where with me in the house," he told the *Observer*. In Book One of the Inheritance Cycle, Eragon is given a magical red sword called Zar'roc.

ADVENTURE CONTINUES WITH *ELDEST*

By the end of 2004, Paolini had finished his book tour for *Eragon* in the United States and the United Kingdom. He returned to his family's home near Livingston, Montana, to start work on his second novel, *Eldest*.

INVENTED LANGUAGES

Author Christopher Paolini invented three languages for the books in his best-selling Inheritance Cycle. The main language is based on Old Norse and is known as the "ancient language."

According to *The Inheritance Almanac* by Michael Macauley, the ancient language is the original language of truth and magic. Those who speak the language cannot lie. Masters of the ancient language can cast spells and make others heed their will. In Paolini's books, elves speak this language. The Dragon Riders were also trained to speak the ancient language. Macauley explains that making a mistake in the language can result in unintended consequences, including death.

The second language Paolini invented is the dwarf language, which he created from scratch. "I love it because it just has such a great guttural sound," Paolini said in an interview with *Boys' Life*. "It was the first sort of language that I created all on my own without referencing anything in the real world."

The Urgal language is the third language the acclaimed author created for his books. "That is the sketchiest of the three," Paolini said in an interview with Bill Thompson of *Eye on Books*. This language is spoken by a brutal, horn-headed race called the Urgals. The language has only a few words, including *drajl*, which means "spawn of maggots."

Paolini said he consulted Old Norse dictionaries, Web sites, and his sister when he created these languages. "My sister and I would talk about stuff, like whether or how the possessives should be formed," he told the *New York Times*. Paolini's books have a glossary to help readers understand the different languages.

The story continues the adventures of Eragon and Saphira. The two travel to the land of elves, where Eragon receives more training in magic and swordsmanship. They face new dangers and treachery as they continue their quest to conquer the evil King Galbatorix.

Eldest opens in the aftermath of a bloody battle. Three days have passed since Eragon and Saphira helped defeat the dark forces sent by Galbatorix. During the brutal clash, Eragon killed a sorcerer named Durza. He plunged his sword, Zar'roc, through the wizard's heart. The battle left Eragon weak and injured. A woman named Angela heals Eragon's wounds. She is a feisty witch and herbalist, whose character is based on Paolini's younger sister, Angela.

"I decided to include a lampoon of my sister, who coincidentally is also named Angela," Paolini wrote on Teenreads.com. "Fortunately for my bodily well-being, she has an excellent sense of humor."

Paolini said he and his sister are so close they can talk in one-word sentences. She is following in her brother's literary footsteps and is an aspiring screenwriter.

ANOTHER PUBLISHING SUCCESS

The second novel in Paolini's Inheritance Cycle arrived in bookstores on August 23, 2005. The much-anticipated *Eldest* became another overnight publishing sensation.

Eldest immediately climbed to the top of *USA TODAY*'s best-selling books list. It became the first book to kick *Harry Potter and the Half-Blood Prince* from the top position. *Eldest* also flew to the number one position on the *Publishers Weekly* and *New York*

Fans flocked to meet Paolini after his second book, *Eldest*, was released in 2005. The book became another international best seller and earned the coveted Quill Book Award in 2006.

Times best-seller lists. It stayed on top of the *New York Times* list for fifty-two weeks.

In its first seven days on the market, more than 425,000 copies of *Eldest* were sold in North America. The 681-page book became the biggest single-week seller in the history of Random House Children's Books. It also became the fastest-selling title in the publisher's history.

ROCK–STAR RECEPTION

Shortly after *Eldest* arrived in bookstores, Paolini hit the road to meet his growing legion of fans. More than two thousand fans, for example, greeted Paolini at a bookstore in Maryland in 2005. "He's treated like a rock star," Carol Memmott of *USA TODAY* reported. "Many of his young fans are standing on tiptoe trying to get a better look. They're holding copies of *Eragon* and *Eldest*. Kids who had waited quietly for several hours, many with their noses in a book, are now hooting and clapping."

Paolini traveled to eighteen states and Canada during his book tour for *Eldest*. In October 2005, he flew to Europe to promote his book in Spain, Germany, Italy, and the United Kingdom.

Eldest later won a coveted award in the publishing industry. It captured the 2006 Quill Book Award in the Young Adult Literature category. This book award is unique because readers choose the winner.

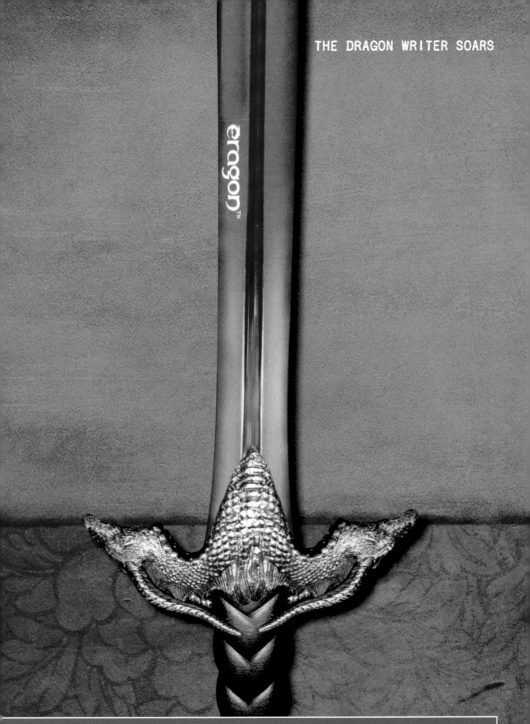

eragon™

One of Eragon's most prized possessions is a magical red sword called Zar'roc. The young dragon rider was given the sword in Book One of Paolini's Inheritance Cycle.

ERAGON SOARS TO THE SILVER SCREEN

Fox 2000 Pictures, a division of 20th Century Fox, made a movie based on Paolini's epic fantasy. "We read the book very early in manuscript form when the family was trying to self-publish it," Elizabeth

Fox 2000 Pictures released the movie *Eragon*, based on Paolini's books, in 2006. *Eragon* featured such stars as Ed Speleers (Eragon) and Rachel Weisz (the voice of Saphira).

Gabler, the president of Fox 2000 Pictures, told *USA TODAY*. "We found the core relationship between a boy and a dragon who share a telepathic connection a strong concept for a movie."

In August 2005, Fox started production of *Eragon* in Budapest, Hungary. The movie featured such stars as Ed Speleers (Eragon), Jeremy Irons

(Brom), John Malkovich (Galbatorix), and Rachel Weisz (the voice of Saphira).

Eragon premiered in theaters across the country on December 15, 2006. It was also shown in theaters around the world. According to the Internet Movie Database, *Eragon* grossed more than $23 million during its opening weekend in the United States. In total, the film made an estimated $250 million around the world.

Paolini applauded Fox's decision to bring *Eragon*'s tale to the silver screen. "I originally conceived *Eragon* as a movie," the author said in a press release. "I saw the characters and action clearly in my mind. But since I didn't have the money to produce a film, I ended up writing the story as a book."

As moviegoers flocked to theaters to see *Eragon*, Paolini headed back to Montana to work on his third book, *Brisingr*. In Old Norse, the word *brisingr* means "fire." It turned out to be the perfect title for Paolini's book, which set the publishing industry on fire.

MORE DRAGON MAGIC

It was almost midnight on September 19, 2008. Author Christopher Paolini couldn't stop smiling as he walked back and forth in front of hundreds of people inside a packed Barnes & Noble bookstore in New York. You could hear the excitement in the twenty-four-year-old writer's voice as he talked about his latest book, *Brisingr*. You could see the enthusiasm in his eyes. In less than three minutes—at 12:01 AM on Saturday, September 20, 2008—the third book in Paolini's best-selling fantasy series would be released.

This was a magical moment for the once unknown teenage writer. It marked the first time in Paolini's career that one of his books would be released at midnight. In the publishing world, a midnight launch

Paolini's third book, *Brisingr*, set the publishing world on fire by selling a record 550,000 copies its first day on the market.

is a sign that an author has made his or her mark on the industry in terms of sales. "Welcome to the official launch of the third book of the Inheritance Cycle, *Brisingr*!" an exuberant Paolini shouted. Cheers erupted from the audience, which included fans dressed as characters from the novelist's dragon-inspired tales. "I can't tell you how happy I am to be here."

Paolini said the release of *Brisingr* marked a major step in his journey as a writer. His quest started in 1998 when he penned the first draft of his international best seller, *Eragon*. Since then, more than 15.5 million copies of *Eragon* and his second book, *Eldest*, had been sold around the world. "This November is going to mark the tenth year that I've been working on this series," Paolini told fans in New York. "So it's

VIRTUAL DRAGON RIDER

Random House, Inc., developed an online game to build up excitement for the release of Christopher Paolini's third book, *Brisingr*. The Vroengard Academy was a virtual world in which players learned how to become legendary Dragon Riders. In the game, players solved clues and puzzles online—in the imaginary land of Alagaësia before the fall of the Dragon Riders—and in the real world.

"I love these sorts of puzzles and games myself," Paolini said shortly after the game's release in June 2008. "So it just seemed like a really cool thing to do to get the news out about *Brisingr* and to get everyone excited about it." The game marked the first time Random House released an alternate reality experience (ARE) to market one of its books.

Fans of the Inheritance Cycle can play other games based on Paolini's books on the author's official Web site, http://www.alagaesia.com. A game called Inheritance Quest came out shortly before the November 2011 release of Paolini's final book in the series, *Inheritance*. Players face more than fifty challenges in this game.

The Web site also has a training arena where players can practice their Dragon Rider skills and even challenge the horn-headed Urgals in a battle called Urgal Combat. Other activities on the Web site include an interactive Alagaësia Adventure Game, trivia questions to test fans knowledge of the books, and an animated map of the mystical world Paolini created for his popular series.

wonderful to be here with you today, to finally have the third book coming out, and to know that all of you are going to get a chance to read it very, very soon."

DRAGON RELEASED INTO THE WILD

After Paolini answered a few questions from the crowd, the witching hour that fans had waited for finally arrived. "It's midnight!" Paolini roared. He gazed at posters of the golden dragon on the book's cover. "And as of now, this gold dragon has just been released into the wild." More than two thousand bookstores nationwide held midnight release parties for *Brisingr*.

The 784-page book continues the mythical tale of Eragon, his blue dragon, Saphira, and their quest to defeat a cruel king and save the empire. "It has lots of battles and villains and romance and swords and dragons, dwarves, and elves," Paolini told New York fans. "Everything a book needs."

RECORD SALES

Brisingr cast a powerful spell on readers. The book sold 550,000 copies during its first day on the market. That is four times as many copies as *Eldest* sold on its first day. *Brisingr* also became the biggest one-day sale ever recorded for a Random House

Children's Books title. The publishing giant printed 2.5 million copies of *Brisingr* in its first run—the largest in the company's history.

Paolini's midnight launch kicked off his nationwide book tour to promote *Brisingr*. He then traveled from New York to California to talk about his latest release. His tour also included a stop in Canada. According to Cecelia Goodnow of the *Seattle Post-Intelligencer*, Paolini read his favorite line in the book to the sold-out crowds that greeted him on his tour. The line is on page 593: "Die, puny human!"

"What's the point of writing fantasy if you can't write lines like, 'Die, puny human'?" he told fans in Seattle.

Paolini wrote one-third of *Brisingr* by hand, using an ink-dip pen. His handwriting is so small that he can fit about two thousand words on a page.

Paolini also explained why he chose *Brisingr* for the title of his novel. "As some of you may know, *brisingr* is actually a word from Old Norse; it means 'fire,'" he told fans in New York. "It's the first magical word that shows up in the series, and it's the first word of magic that Eragon uses. It saves his life, actually." Eragon first speaks the word "brisingr" when he shoots and kills a monstrous Urgal with a fiery arrow.

WRITING WITH QUILL AND INK

During his ten-city book tour, Paolini discussed the challenges he faced writing *Brisingr*. The book took him two and a half years to finish, he said. His words didn't flow as easily as they did with his other novels. His confidence was shaken. "I was obsessing over every single word," he told the *Seattle Post-Intelligencer*. "It got to the point where I was having trouble finishing a single page in a day."

Paolini decided to try a different approach to writing. He turned off his computer and picked up a quill, a bottle of ink, and parchment paper. His words started to flow again. His confidence returned.

Paolini wrote one-third of *Brisingr* by hand. "I had a blast doing it," he said in an interview on the *Today Show*. "The only problem with it is that I write so small, I ended up putting about two thousand words on a page. And my mom was typing the pages in for me. She complained she was going to go blind trying to read my writing."

Paolini also wrote *Brisingr* from different points of view, including telling some chapters through the eyes of his favorite character, Saphira. "I was actually a little nervous when I got up to that [point] because I knew that unless I could do it perfectly, it wasn't worth doing at all because she's so important to the series," Paolini told fans in New York.

TRILOGY BECOMES CYCLE

As he wrote *Brisingr*, Paolini faced another daunting challenge. The third book was originally supposed to end the series. The author, however, discovered he needed more words to finish his epic saga. Paolini told Meredith Vieira of the *Today Show*, "I realized it [*Brisingr*] was going to be two thousand pages long if I finished the story with it, so I decided to split it into two volumes. And I think that was the best thing to do for the series."

His publisher agreed. "Christopher has really grown as a writer," Nancy Hinkel, vice president and publishing director of Knopf, said in a statement announcing that Paolini's trilogy would become a four-book cycle. "And the next two books promise to deliver even more of his signature heart-stopping adventure, as well as thrilling revelations about the

Paolini worked with editor Michelle Frey on all four books in his popular Inheritance Cycle. She cut twenty thousand words from his original *Eragon* manuscript but didn't change the story line.

characters whom fans around the world have come to love."

Paolini's instincts as a storyteller paid off. *Brisingr* set the literary world on fire. The book quickly rose to the number one spot on the *New York Times*, *USA TODAY*, and *Publishers Weekly* lists. It became the fastest-selling title in the company's history, too. By early 2011, *Eragon*, *Eldest*, and *Brisingr* had collectively sold more than twenty-five million copies around the world.

THE BEGINNING OF THE END

The three-time best-selling author returned to Montana to write the final installment in his Inheritance Cycle. Paolini, however, no longer lived in his small boyhood farmhouse along the Yellowstone River. The millionaire writer and his family now lived in what Matthew Brown of the *Associated Press* called a "sprawling residence" in a more isolated part of Paradise Valley.

Paolini has a private wing in the house. "I just need a few square feet to sleep in, a quiet place to write, a place to do exercise, and good food," Paolini told Brown. "And I've got good food here."

On March 23, 2011, Knopf announced the title for the long-awaited final book in Paolini's series: *Inheritance*. Paolini released an "official video" to celebrate the moment he finished *Inheritance*. The

video opens with a shot of the novelist sitting cross-legged on a couch in his home office. It cuts to a tight shot of Paolini typing the words "THE END" on his laptop computer.

"I just typed the last few words—paragraph—of Book Four of the Inheritance Cycle," Paolini says in the video. "I'm having trouble actually putting any of this into words because I've been working on this book and this series for so long, I can't even really wrap my head around the fact that it's actually—it's done. I just wrote it. It's done! The end."

In the video, Paolini explains that *Inheritance* was the hardest book in the series for him to write.

aolini joined fans in New York to celebrate the November 2011 release of *Inheritance*, the final installment in his acclaimed series. *Inheritance* sold nearly ve hundred thousand copies on its first day.

He also calls it the best book in the series. "The characters really go through the ringer in this one, in a good way," he says.

ALL IS REVEALED

Paolini promised fans that all their burning questions would be answered in the final book in the series. Those answers were finally revealed when *Inheritance* arrived in bookstores on November 8, 2011—nine days before Paolini's twenty-eighth birthday. "This is both a thrilling and gratifying end to a wonderful journey that began more than a decade ago," Paolini said in a written statement.

Paolini's fans flocked to bookstores to get their hands on the final installment of the young writer's epic fantasy. Random House Children's Books listed the official first-day sales at 489,500 copies in print, digital, and audio—a figure the company said marked the highest first-day sale of any book published in 2011.

Inheritance quickly rose to the top of best-sellers lists. Two days after it arrived in bookstores, *Inheritance* had knocked off Walter Isaacson's biography, *Steve Jobs*, from the number one spot on Amazon's best-sellers list. The book also debuted at the top of *USA TODAY*'s list.

Random House printed 2.5 million copies of *Inheritance* in its first run of the anticipated best seller. It launched a nationwide marketing campaign that included advertisements about *Inheritance* in movie theaters, television, and newspapers. The campaign also included an eighteen-city book tour by Paolini in the United States, as well as travel and book promotion in the United Kingdom. "It's been an amazing ride from start to finish," Paolini told the *Seattle Post-Intelligencer*.

Paolini said he planned to take a "bit of a break" after he finished his Inheritance Cycle. He wanted to catch up on his reading. And, of course, the magical storyteller planned to continue weaving tales that would cast a spell on readers for years to come.

During an interview on the *Today Show*, Paolini even laid down the gauntlet for a personal writing challenge. "I want to try as a test for myself to see if I can write three to four short to medium-length stories, novellas, books, back-to-back in a couple of months," he said. "I don't know if I can do it, but I really want to try."

As the characters said in *Eragon*: "May your swords stay sharp."

FIVE

SECRETS OF MAGICAL WRITING

Christopher Paolini never thought he would write a best-selling novel when he picked up his pen to start *Eragon*. He never dreamed the words he wrote at fifteen would become what *People* magazine hailed as "literary magic." Paolini didn't use any literary spells or incantations early in his writing career. He didn't know any when he started. The magic that poured from Paolini's pen came much later. He first had to be trained as a dragon writer.

"I had absolutely no idea what I was doing in the beginning," Paolini wrote in an essay on BookBrowse.com. "It never occurred to me that I might actually be a professional writer one day. All I really wanted to do was share the epics floating around in my head with other people—writing was just something I had to master in order to make those sagas reality."

DRAGON WRITER TRAINING

To master his writing skills, the precocious author did what he does best. He studied. He read. He wrote and rewrote. He worked tirelessly for hours every day. And he tried to learn everything he could about the craft of writing.

"When I was thirteen and fourteen, I made several stabs at writing down some of the epics I constantly daydreamed about," Paolini wrote on Teenreads.com. "However, they always petered out after five or ten pages, mainly because I didn't know what should happen next with the characters. I realized that I needed to learn how to construct strong plots that could be sustained over the course of an entire novel."

Paolini started reading books about the art of writing. He delved into chapters about plot, story arc, and structure. He turned to *The Writer's Handbook*, Orson Scott Card's *Characters and Viewpoints*, and Robert McKee's *Story* for guidance. The budding author also ran through a series of literary exercises. He drafted a nine-page summary for a fantasy novel. "The exercise provided me with much needed experience and confidence," Paolini wrote on Teenreads.com.

Author Philip Pullman is one of Christopher Paolini's favorite writers. Paolini said he studied Pullman's books, including the epic trilogy His Dark Materials, before he wrote *Eragon*.

In his next literary exercise, Paolini hammered out a detailed outline for a much longer book. The first sparks of his magical writing became etched in those words. Paolini used that outline to plot his first three books. "For weeks, I struggled to figure out every detail," he wrote on BookBrowse.com. The outline and plot became invaluable guides on his writing quest, Paolini said. They kept his story on track and helped him make sure he wasn't "writing blindly."

The writing exercises also helped Paolini flesh out the elements he wanted in his books. As he wrote on BookBrowse.com, he made sure to include "an intelligent, questioning hero; lavish descriptions; exotic locations; dragons; elves; dwarves; magic; and above all else, a sense of awe and wonder."

OTHER TEEN AUTHORS

Christopher Paolini isn't the only teenager to become a best-selling author. Here are other famous young authors:

- **Mary Shelley** wrote the horror novel *Frankenstein* before she was nineteen. The book was her third published work. Some people say the English author changed the plot of *Frankenstein* after the death of her first child.

- **Anne Frank** was thirteen when she started writing her diary. She wrote the diary while she and her Jewish family were hiding from the Nazis in the Netherlands. Her family was later betrayed, and Anne died in a concentration camp at the age of fifteen. Her father, the only family member who survived, published his daughter's diary, *The Diary of Anne Frank*.

- **Amelia Atwater-Rhodes** wrote her first novel, *In The Forests of the Night*, at the age of thirteen. Her second novel is *Demon in the Eyes*. She was selected by *Teen People* magazine as one of "20 Teens Who Will Change the World."

- **S. E. Hinton** wrote her first book, *The Outsiders*, when she was sixteen. After the book's release, the Oklahoma native became known as "the Voice of the Youth." She wrote several other books for young adults, including *Rumble Fish*, *Tex*, and *Hawkes Harbor*. Some schools have banned her books.

- **Ned Vizzini** was nineteen when his book *Teen Angst? Naaah* was published. The award-winning author later wrote other books for young adults, including *Be More Chill* and *It's Kind of a Funny Story*.

STUDYING MASTER STORYTELLERS

The dragon writer's training wasn't finished, though. Before he picked up his mighty pen, Paolini studied books written by his favorite authors, including J. R. R. Tolkien (*Lord of the Rings*), David Eddings (*The Ruby Knight*), E. R. Eddison (*The Worm Ouroboros*), Frank Herbert (*Dune*), Anne McCaffrey (The Dragonriders of Pern), and Philip Pullman (His Dark Materials).

Paolini also researched Norse mythology and Seamus Heaney's translation of *Beowulf*, an epic poem about a Scandinavian warrior. Paolini kept a copy of the poem by his bed.

"He read with renewed interest the *Beowulf* saga and found similarities between it and Tolkien's *Hobbit* and *Lord of the Rings*," Paolini's mother, Talita, wrote in *Home Education Magazine*. "He pondered the threads that wove through these stories and more contemporary ones such as *Star Wars*. And he searched for his own expression of the archetypal heroic young-man-coming-of-age adventure story."

TREMULOUS PEN TO PAPER

The day finally arrived when Paolini was ready to test his newfound skills. He was fifteen when he put his "tremulous pen to paper" and started *Eragon*. "I worked sporadically at first, but as I became more and more engaged with my project, I spent as much time as I could writing," he wrote in an essay on Teenreads.com.

Paolini penned the first sixty pages by hand. At the time, the teenage writer was still learning to type. According to *Weekly Reader*, Paolini listened to classical music by such composers as Wagner, Mahler, and Beethoven while he worked. He wrote the final battle scene in *Eragon* while listening to *Carmina Burana* by Carl Orff.

Paolini said the words and images in *Eragon* flowed from his hands. "Part of my speed was due to the fact that I had no idea what, technically, constituted good writing, and therefore, I did not edit myself during this process," he wrote in his essay.

Paolini often listens to classical music when he writes. He wrote the final battle scene in *Eragon* while listening to Carl Orff's popular classical piece *Carmina Burana*, performed above by the Fine Arts Opera and Orchestra of Mexico.

It took Paolini a year to finish his first draft of *Eragon*. In this version of the story, the Dragon Rider's name was Kevin instead of Eragon, according to *The Inheritance Almanac*. Paolini later changed his protagonist's name and rewrote other parts of his book, which he considered a work in progress. "I was dismayed by how amateurish it seemed," Paolini wrote of his first draft. "The story was fine, but it was mired in atrocious language and grammar. I was like a musician who has composed his first aria, only to discover that he can't perform it because he has not yet learned to sing."

Paolini and his family spent the next two years editing and fine-tuning *Eragon*. Those days became the most difficult chapters in Paolini's writing journey. On BookBrowse.com, Paolini said editing the book felt like "splinters of hot bamboo being driven into my tender eyeballs." He described the editing process as "excruciating" in an interview with the *Missoulian*. "It was awful because you think you've fixed something, think you've done it right, and you're constantly being told your best effort is wrong," he said. "That lasted a year, and it was like being tied to a rack and tortured with thumbscrews."

Paolini closed that painful chapter in 2001 when his family self-published *Eragon*. His father formatted the book in Adobe PageMaker for publication. He also determined what the chapter titles should look like, how the cover should be designed, and many other details.

MARKETING MASTERS

Paolini and his parents focused their attention on another skill that writers must master: marketing and promotion. Paolini and his father spent a year traveling across the country to promote *Eragon*. "We started by doing book signings in bookstores but quickly learned that no one shows up for an author they have never heard of," Paolini said in *The Making of a Bestseller* by Brian Hill and Dee Power.

The struggling author often stayed in the stores for hours. He talked to every person who came through the doors. "On a good day, I might sell forty books," he said. "That's not bad for a signing, but it's a lot of work."

To help market the book, the Paolinis designed an educational program around *Eragon* for school-children. "I then learned that if I went into a school and did a presentation, in one day we could sell 300 books or more, and inspire students to read and write," he said in *The Making of a Bestseller*. "We also started charging a fee for the presentation, to help cover travel expenses." The Paolinis tweaked their marketing strategy and began to focus more on these school visits.

Paolini mastered another marketing skill. He became an excellent salesman. "I remember one time I actually sold a copy of *Eragon* to a guy who didn't read English," he said in an interview with Matthew Peterson of TheAuthorHour.com. (He convinced the man to buy it as a gift for his girlfriend.) Paolini and his family sold approximately ten thousand copies of *Eragon*. They made some of those sales out of the back of the family's van.

USING WHAT HE LEARNED

Paolini's breakout moment came in 2003 when publisher Alfred A. Knopf released its version of *Eragon*. The nineteen-year-old writer became an instant best-selling author. The fantasy novelist, however, never forgot the lessons he learned as a younger writer. He channeled the skills that made "literary magic" in *Eragon* when he wrote the other books in his acclaimed Inheritance Cycle—*Eldest*, *Brisingr*, and *Inheritance*.

Paolini, for example, still used his original outline as a guide on his writing quest. He updated it over the years as his story developed. By the time he started work on *Brisingr*, Paolini's outline was fourteen pages long.

The author continued to write consistently every day from his Montana home. "I get bolts of inspiration about once every three months," he told

Christopher Paolini's Inheritance Cycle may be finished, but he plans to continue writing and meeting with his fans. Paolini often reminds his readers to follow their dreams and never give up.

Peterson. "And between those bolts of inspiration the writing, while enjoyable, is definitely work. And I just treat it like a job. Every day I get up, I sit down, and I work on the book. So being consistent will get you a lot further than just waiting for bolts of white-hot inspiration."

Paolini listened to classical music as he penned his sequels, too. He also wrote most of his novels on an Apple computer. The wordsmith, however, composed some sections of his books in a cloth-bound notebook. "I get out my inkwell and pen and pull out the notebook," he told the *Missoulian*. "I pick the right nib, dip my pen in, and start writing very slowly." Paolini wrote one-third of *Brisingr* with an ink-dip pen.

NEVER GIVE UP

As the popularity of his books skyrocketed, Paolini never forgot his fans. He stayed connected with them. He took time to answer their questions. And he always shared the secrets he learned as a young writer.

"Write about what you enjoy the most or what touches you the most, otherwise you'll never be able to endure a book-length project," he said in an interview with *Time For Kids*.

In the interview with Matthew Peterson for TheAuthorHour.com, Paolini said aspiring writers must also be well read. "Read everything you can get your hands on," he said. Paolini has read several thousand books. "Reading is probably the single most important skill I've learned in my life," he told *Boys' Life* magazine.

During an interview with Teenreads.com, Paolini said writers must also be persistent, disciplined, and open to constructive criticism in order to achieve excellence. "Writing is a craft, and, like any craft, you must practice, practice, practice to hone your skills," he said.

Paolini also reminded writers to never become discouraged. "If you're an aspiring writer, I think the best thing that I could say to you is never, ever, ever, ever give up," he said in a video released by Random House.

The dragon writer never gave up his quest. If he had, there would be a lot less magic in the world.

ON CHRISTOPHER PAOLINI

Date of birth: November 17, 1983

Birthplace: Southern California

Currently resides: Paradise Valley, Montana

Boyhood home: Paradise Valley, Montana. He moved there from Anchorage, Alaska, when he was eight.

First publication: Self-published *Eragon* in November 2001 through his family's small publishing company, Paolini International, LLC. New York publisher Alfred A. Knopf released its version of *Eragon* on August 26, 2003.

Other books: *Eldest* (Knopf, 2005), *Brisingr* (Knopf, 2008), *Inheritance* (Knopf, 2011). Paolini also wrote *Eragon's Guide to Alagaësia*, which Knopf released in 2009.

Movie based on his work: *Eragon* (Fox 2000 Pictures, December 2006)

Marital status: Single

Parents: Kenneth and Talita Paolini

Siblings: One younger sister, Angela

Height: 5'8"

Education: Paolini was homeschooled by his parents. He graduated at the age of fifteen from the American School, an accredited distance-learning program in Lansing, Illinois. He has taken online college courses and was accepted to Reed College in Portland, Oregon.

Hobbies: Hiking, camping, yoga, weight lifting, reading, watching movies, playing computer games, painting, drawing, and making knives, swords, and chain mail.

Fears: Heights, falling, being cut, and hearing growls in the darkness.

Interesting facts: Paolini is color-blind and sees mostly shades of blue; he built a Hobbit house with an eight-foot tunnel near his boyhood home in Montana; he doesn't like fast food restaurants.

ON CHRISTOPHER PAOLINI'S WORK

Eragon (Self-published version)

Publisher: Paolini International, LLC

Released: November 2001

Summary: A poor fifteen-year-old farm boy named Eragon finds a mysterious blue stone in the forest. He hopes he can sell it to buy food for his family. The stone, however, turns out to be a dragon's egg. After a brilliant blue dragon hatches, Eragon discovers that he is a legendary Dragon Rider. The revelation changes his simple life overnight. Armed with his faithful dragon, Saphira, an ancient red sword, and advice from an old storyteller, Eragon embarks on a vengeful quest to save the Empire from an evil king. His journey takes him into a world filled with mystical creatures, dark magic, and bloody battles.

Sales: Paolini and his family sold about ten thousand copies of the book. Paolini visited more than 135 schools, libraries, and bookstores nationwide to promote the book. Copies of the self-published *Eragon* are now collector's items that sell for hundreds of dollars.

Eragon

Publisher: Alfred A. Knopf

Released: August 26, 2003

Summary: Knopf cut twenty thousand words from Paolini's self-published version of the book but did not change the story line. The fate of the Empire rests with Eragon and his magical dragon, Saphira. Can they defeat the wicked King Galbatorix and his dark forces? Can Eragon live up to his legacy as a Dragon Rider? *Eragon* is the first installment in Paolini's four-book Inheritance Cycle.

Sales: Knopf printed one hundred thousand copies of *Eragon* in its first run. Six months after its release, one million copies of the book were in print. By 2011, there were over fifty foreign-language licenses for *Eragon*. *Eragon* debuted at number three on the *New York Times* best-seller list for children's chapter books. Within months, the book soared to the number one position on the *New York Times*, *USA TODAY*, and *Publishers Weekly* best-seller lists. It held the top spot on the *New York Times* list for twenty-six consecutive weeks. *Eragon* also became an internationally best-selling novel.

Movie adaption: Fox 2000 Pictures made a motion picture based on Paolini's novel. *Eragon* hit the silver screen in theaters across the country on December 15, 2006. Filmed in Budapest, Hungary, the movie grossed $23 million its opening weekend. Around the world, *Eragon* the movie made an estimated $250 million.

Eldest

Publisher: Alfred A. Knopf
Published: August 23, 2005
Summary: After helping the rebel state defeat the dark
forces sent by King Galbatorix, Eragon travels to the
land of elves for more training as a Dragon Rider. He
must master two vital skills: magic and swordsmanship. As Eragon and Saphira continue their quest to
overcome the evil king, they face even more danger,
chaos, and betrayal. Back at home in Carvahall,
Eragon's cousin, Roran, is fighting a new battle. It's
a fight that puts Eragon in even more danger.
Sales: *Eldest* sold more than 425,000 copies in its first
days on the market in North America. It later sold
millions of copies around the world. *Eldest* became
a number one best seller on the *USA TODAY*,
Publishers Weekly, and *New York Times* lists. It
held the top spot on the *New York Times* list for
fifty-two weeks. It was also a *Wall Street Journal*
best-selling book.
Awards: 2006 Quill Book Award; Book Sense Book of
the Year for 2006.

Brisingr

Publisher: Alfred A. Knopf
Released: September 20, 2008
Summary: Eragon and Saphira barely escape with
their lives in a bloody battle against the Empire's
warriors on the Burning Plains. More adventures
and danger, however, lie ahead for the young rider
and his magical dragon. They find themselves

wrapped up in a web of promises they might not be able to keep. Eragon vows to help Roran rescue Katrina from the monstrous Ra'zac. But the young Dragon Rider also has loyalties to others. Eragon is ultimately faced with a choice that may force him to make an unimaginable sacrifice in his quest to defeat King Galbatorix.

Sales: *Brisingr* sold 550,000 hardcover copies on its first day. By early 2011, *Eragon*, *Eldest*, and *Brisingr* had collectively sold more than twenty-five million copies around the world. *Brisingr* became a number one best seller on the *New York Times*, *USA TODAY*, and *Publishers Weekly* lists. Knopf printed 2.5 million copies of *Brisingr* in its first run—the largest first printing in its history.

Inheritance

Publisher: Alfred A. Knopf

Released: November 8, 2011

Summary: Eragon has endured months of training in his journey as a young Dragon Rider and Shadeslayer. He and his dragon, Saphira, have engaged in many bloody battles in their quest to defeat the evil King Galbatorix. Their victories have given hope to the Empire. But they've also brought painful losses. In the conclusion of Paolini's internationally best-selling series, Eragon and Saphira face their most dangerous battle. They must confront Galbatorix. But can they defeat him and restore peace to the Empire? And if they can, what price will they ultimately pay?

Sales: Knopf printed 2.5 million copies of *Inheritance* in its first run. The book sold nearly five hundred thousand copies on its first day.

Eragon's Guide to Alagaësia

Publisher: Alfred A. Knopf

Released: November 3, 2009

Summary: The book is an illustrated guide to the magical people, places, and creatures in the imaginary land of Alagaësia. Eragon, the young Dragon Rider, is the narrator.

Sales: The book was ranked number 26,270 on Amazon's best-seller list in September 2011.

Eragon (2003)

"This solid, sweeping epic fantasy crosses vast geography as it follows 15-year-old Eragon from anonymous farm boy to sword-wielding icon...A slight tone of arrogance running through the narrative voice will hardly bother readers busily enjoying the reliable motifs of elegant immortal elves, mining dwarves, a wise elderly man, and a hero of mysterious birth." — *Kirkus Reviews*, July 15, 2003

"[An] impressive epic fantasy. The fantasy bildungsroman has the brave youngster learning about exile, magic, love and his own destiny, and Paolini promises his saga will continue in two more volumes of the planned Inheritance series." — *Publishers Weekly*, April 4, 2005

"*Eragon* by science fiction and fantasy enthusiast Christopher Paolini is a vigorously written high fantasy epic...*Eragon* is highly recommended for dedicated fantasy enthusiasts." — *Midwest Book Review*

Eldest (2005)

"Eragon continues his Rider training in this dense sequel. Suffused with purple prose and faux-archaic language, this patchwork of dialogue, characters and concepts pulled whole cloth from the fantasy canon holds together remarkably well. Dramatic

CRITICAL REVIEWS

tension is maintained through the interweaving of Eragon's and Roran's adventures...Derivative but exciting." — *Kirkus Reviews*

"Surpassing its popular prequel *Eragon*, this second volume in the Inheritance trilogy shows growing maturity and skill on the part of its very young author, who was only seventeen when the first volume was published in 2003." — Amazon

"Readers who persevere are rewarded with walloping revelations in the final pages...The story leaves off with a promise...To Be Continued." — *Publishers Weekly*

"It's clear that Paolini has drive and talent, and *Eldest* is, for the most part, competently constructed and written. The problem, however, is that anyone committed to reading a 2,000-page epic deserves more than competence and tropes that have been used countless times before." — Michael Berry, *San Francisco Chronicle*, October 9, 2005

Brisingr (2008)

"The clichéd journey may appeal to younger readers of genre fiction. Older teens, even those who might have first cut their teeth on Paolini's writing years ago, are less likely to be impressed." — *Publishers Weekly*, September 22, 2008

"Had I read this novel when I was 13, it would have kept me up straight through the night. For that matter, I might have even stolen a few bits from it for D&D (Dungeons and Dragons). And that's a compliment." — David Anthony Durham, *Washington Post*, September 25, 2008

"Paolini plainly enjoys wandering around in his fantasy world, and patient fans of Tolkien and similar writers will not begrudge him his leisurely progress. Others might wish for a clearer story arc." — Kathleen Beck, *VOYA*

Eragon's Guide to Alagaësia (2009)

"This eye-catching interactive companion book to Paolini's Inheritance Cycle is designed to provide newly elected Dragon Riders with background about the world of Alagaësia. A map and drawings of the natural terrain provide mise en scène, while flaps reveal mini narratives, and envelopes contain personal notes written by Eragon Shadeslayer. A time line of formative events, like the beginning of the Dragon War, and a taxonomy of Alagaësia inhabitants—humans, elves, dragons, and numerous

species of animals—will intrigue enthusiasts."
— *Publishers Weekly*, December 14, 2009

"Designed in the style of such books as *Ernest Drake's Dragonology* (Candlewick, 2003), this large, colorful, well-illustrated volume has many foldouts and removable pieces. The cover, which looks as if it were bound in the scaly blue skin of Eragon's dragon, Saphira, adds a slightly creepy touch."
— Walter Minkel, *School Library Journal*, January 1, 2010

Inheritance (2009)

"It is an extremely compelling and well written book, set in the magical land of Alagaësia, and is one of the best fantasy books I have read. Christopher Paolini is a great author who has been able to conjure up a fantastical yet believable world. This is just as brilliant as all the other books in the series and ends spectacularly, but not in the way I expected." — *Guardian*, December 1, 2011

"Adventurers, take up ye swords! Several of the battle scenes in this massive conclusion to Paolini's Inheritance Cycle—and, wow, are there a lot of them—are so invigorating that even with all the fountaining of blood and clashing of steel, readers young and old will be begging to enlist…Paolini fulfills nearly every promise set forward in Eragon (2003), with the young Rider fulfilling his destiny; Roran becoming a warrior of legend; Murtagh facing up to his lineage; and Galbatorix finally taking center stage for the final act, where his evil plans begin to make a disturbing amount of sense. — Booklist Online, November 9, 2011

"In full Tolkienesque style, Paolini luxuriates in excess details, side quests, and a lengthy dénouement in which every last thread is wrapped up. The solidly entertaining plot is fleshed out with defining moments for every major character and a sense of completion (temporary or permanent) for all involved. While this final chapter is bogged down by an almost obsessive complexity with regard to the world-building, Paolini leaves readers with the satisfaction of a journey's end, along with the promise of new beginnings. It's a can't-miss for fans and completionists, and a worthy end to the story." — *Publisher's Weekly*, November 7, 2011

1983 Christopher Paolini is born on November 17 in Southern California. His family later moves to Anchorage, Alaska.

1991 Paolini's family moves to Paradise Valley, Montana.

1998 Paolini graduates from high school at the age of fifteen after completing a distance-learning program.

1998 Paolini starts writing the first draft of *Eragon*.

1999 Paolini finishes the first draft of *Eragon*.

2000 Paolini finishes the second draft of *Eragon*.

2001 Paolini's family self-publishes *Eragon* through Paolini International, LLC. He spends the next two years traveling across the country to promote his epic fantasy.

2002 Novelist Carl Hiaasen's twelve-year-old stepson reads *Eragon*. Hiaasen recommends *Eragon* to his New York publisher.

2002 Publisher Alfred A. Knopf signs a three-book deal with Paolini that is reportedly worth six figures.

2003 Knopf releases its version of *Eragon* on August 26. Eragon debuts at number three on the *New York Times* best-seller list.

2004 One million copies of *Eragon* are in print by February. The book has also soared to the top of the *New York Times*, *USA TODAY*, and *Publishers Weekly* best-seller lists. Paolini starts work on his second book, *Eldest*.

2005 Knopf releases *Eldest* on August 23. In its first seven days on the market, more than 425,000 copies of *Eldest* are sold in North America. *Eldest* claims the number one position on the *USA TODAY*,

Publishers Weekly, and *New York Times* best-seller lists. It becomes the first book to kick *Harry Potter and the Half-Blood Prince* from the top spot.

2005 Fox 2000 Pictures starts production of the movie adaption of *Eragon* on August 1.

2006 Fox 2000 Pictures releases the movie *Eragon* on December 15. The film grosses $23 million during its opening weekend in the United States.

2006 *Eldest* wins a 2006 Quill Book Award in the Young Adult Literature category. It is also named a Book Sense Book of the Year.

2007 Paolini announces his Inheritance Trilogy will become the four-book Inheritance Cycle.

2008 Knopf releases *Brisingr* at 12:01 AM on September 20. The book sells 550,000 copies its first day on the market. Knopf prints 2.5 million copies of *Brisingr* in its first run—the largest in the history of Random House Children's Books. The book becomes another number one best seller for Paolini.

2009 Knopf releases *Eragon's Guide to Alagaësia* by Paolini. The book is an illustrated guide to the magical people, places, and creatures in the imaginary land of Alagaësia.

2011 In March, Knopf announces the final book in Paolini's Inheritance Cycle will be called *Inheritance*. Knopf releases *Inheritance* on November 8. The publisher prints 2.5 million copies of *Inheritance* in its first run of the anticipated best seller. *Eragon*, *Eldest*, and *Brisingr* have collectively sold more than 25 million copies around the world.

GLOSSARY

ACCREDITED To officially recognize a person or an organization that meets specific standards.

ARCHETYPAL Relating to a model or pattern that is repeated in numerous cultural works.

ATROCIOUS Of very poor quality.

CREDENCE The quality of being believed or accepted as true.

CULT A group that holds religious or spiritual beliefs that many consider extreme, misguided, or false.

EPIC A work of literature that recounts the deeds of a legendary hero.

FORMATIVE Important or influential, especially in shaping or developing a person's character.

GAUNTLET An open challenge.

GUTTURAL Pronounced in the throat or the back of the mouth.

INCANTATION Words spoken or chanted that supposedly will cast a magic spell.

LADEN Carrying a load.

LAMPOON A piece of writing or drawing that mocks a person.

MONTESSORI A method of teaching started in 1907 by Dr. Maria Montessori, the first woman in Italy to become a physician. Her educational methods are based on scientific observations of the processes children use to learn.

MYSTIC Something that has magical properties or is mysterious.

NIB The writing point of a pen, especially the insertable metal part of a fountain pen or dip pen.

PHENOMENON Somebody or something that is rare, extraordinary, or exceptional.

PRECOCIOUS Showing maturity and adult abilities at an unusually early age.

PRODIGY A person with exceptional talent at an early age.

PROFOUND Very deeply and intensely felt; extending to the depths of one's being.

PROTAGONIST The main character in a novel, play, or other literary work.

RUSTIC Relating to the country; rural.

SINGE To burn lightly, especially along the surface, edge, or tip.

TELEPATHIC Involving communication from one mind to another without speech or signs.

TREACHERY An act of betrayal of trust.

TREMULOUS Affected with trembling or shaking.

WERECAT A creature of folklore and fantasy, similar to a werewolf, that takes the form of a feline instead of a wolf.

American Library Association (ALA)
50 E. Huron
Chicago IL 60611
(800) 545-2433
Web site: http://www.ala.org
The American Library Association can help readers find books that match their interests. For example, it can provide recommended reading lists for those who like fantasy novels. The association has also compiled an extensive list of Web sites for students.

Library of Congress
101 Independence Avenue SE
Washington, DC 20540
Web site: http://www.loc.gov
The Library of Congress is the largest library in the world. It has more than 33 million books, 12.5 million photographs, and 64.5 million manuscripts. Its "Ask A Librarian" service provides research assistance on various topics, including authors and their works. Librarians respond to questions within five days.

Random House Children's Books
1745 Broadway
New York, NY 10019
(212) 782-9000
Web site: http://www.randomhouse.com/teens
Random House publishes many of America's most popular and highly acclaimed authors for young

people, including Christopher Paolini and Carl Hiaasen. The Random House Children's Books Web site offers an array of materials and activities free of charge for children, teens, parents, and educators. Fans can write to Christopher Paolini in care of editor Michelle Frey.

Science Fiction and Fantasy Writers of America (SFWA)
P.O. Box 3238
Enfield, CT 06083-3238
Web site: http://www.sfwa.org
The Science Fiction and Fantasy Writers of America is an organization for authors of science fiction, fantasy, and related genres. Past and present members include Isaac Asimov, Anne McCaffrey, Ray Bradbury, and Andre Norton.

SF Canada
7433 East River Road
Washago, ON L0K 2B0
Canada
Web site: http://www.sfcanada.org
SF Canada is an organization for professional writers of speculative fiction, which includes science fiction, fantasy, and other works that "invoke a sense of wonder." The organization provides information about Canadian writers and their works.

Society of Children's Book Writers & Illustrators (SCBWI)
8271 Beverly Boulevard
Los Angeles, CA 90048

(323) 782-1010
Web site: http://www.scbwi.org
The Society of Children's Book Writers & Illustrators is
an organization for writers and illustrators of
children's and young adult literature. The group
has chapters around the world whose members
share ideas, information, and tips about children's
literature.

Society for Creative Anachronism (SCA)
P.O. Box 360789
Milpitas, CA 95036-0789
(800) 789-7486
Web site: http://www.sca.org
The Society for Creative Anachronism is an international
organization that researches and re-creates the
arts and skills practiced in pre-seventeenth-
century Europe. Members dress in clothing from
the Middle Ages and Renaissance and attend
events that feature tournaments, royal courts, and
feasts, as well as various classes and workshops.

WEB SITES

Due to the changing nature of Internet links, Rosen
Publishing has developed an online list of Web sites
related to the subject of this book. This site is updated
regularly. Please use this link to access the list:

http://www.rosenlinks.com/AAA/Paol

Bankston, John. *Christopher Paolini* (Who Wrote That?). New York, NY: Chelsea House, 2011.

Campbell, Joseph. *The Hero's Journey: Joseph Campbell on His Life and Work*. Novato, CA: New World Library, 2003.

Card, Orson Scott. *Characters & Viewpoints: The Elements of Fiction Writing*. Cincinnati, OH: Writer's Digest, 1988.

Card, Orson Scott. *The Writer's Digest Guide to Science Fiction & Fantasy*. Cincinnati, OH: Writer's Digest Books, 2010.

Cotta Vaz, Mark. *Mythic Vision: The Making of* Eragon. New York, NY: Alfred A. Knopf, 2006.

Coville, Bruce. *Jeremy Thatcher, Dragon Hatcher*. San Diego, CA: Jane Yolen Books, 1991.

Eddison, Eric Rücker. *The Worm Ouroboros*. Charleston, SC: Forgotten Books, 2008.

Gresh, Lois H. *The Ultimate Unauthorized* Eragon *Guide: The Hidden Facts Behind the World of Alagaësia*. New York, NY: St. Martin's Griffin, 2006.

Heaney, Seamus, trans. *Beowulf: An Illustrated Edition*. New York, NY: W.W. Norton, 2008.

Herbert, Frank. *Dune*. Philadelphia, PA: Chilton Books, 1965.

Levine, Gail Carson. *Writing Magic: Creating Stories That Fly*. New York, NY: Collins, 2006.

Marcus, Leonard S., ed. *The Wand in the Word: Conversations with Writers of Fantasy*. Somerville, MA: Candlewick Press, 2006.

McCaffrey, Anne. *The Dragonriders of Pern*. New York, NY: Ballantine, 1988.

Owen, James A., and Leah Wilson. *Secrets of the Dragon Riders: Your Favorite Authors on Christopher Paolini's Inheritance Cycle*. Dallas, TX: BenBella Books: Distributed by Perseus Distribution, 2008.

Paolini, Christopher. *Brisingr*. New York, NY: Alfred A. Knopf, 2008.

Paolini, Christopher. *Eldest*. New York, NY: Alfred A. Knopf, 2005.

Paolini, Christopher. *Eragon*. New York, NY: Alfred A. Knopf, 2003.

Paolini, Christopher, Jonathan Lambert, Emma Goldhawk, and Fred Gambino. *Eragon's Guide to Alagaësia*. New York, NY: Alfred A. Knopf, 2009.

Paolini, Christopher. *Inheritance*. New York, NY: Alfred A. Knopf, 2011.

Pullman, Philip. *The Golden Compass*. New York, NY: Alfred A. Knopf, 1996.

Tolkien, J.R.R. *The Hobbit*; *The Lord of the Rings*. Illustrated ed. London, England: HarperCollins, 2010.

Vogler, Christopher. *The Writer's Journey: Mythic Structure for Writers*. 3rd ed. Studio City, CA: Michael Wiese Productions, 2007.

"Ask a Celebrity: Christopher Paolini." *Weekly Reader*, 2010. Retrieved August 31, 2011 (http://64.251. 206.115/wys/christopher.asp).

Associated Press. "Final 'Inheritance' Novel Has Big Opening Day." *Times-Standard*, November 10, 2011. Retrieved December 1, 2011 (http://www. times-standard.com/ci_19307442?source= most_viewed).

"Best-Selling Author Sees Value in Libraries." *Wyoming Library Roundup*, 2008. Retrieved September 1, 2011 (http://ilovelibraries.org/news/topstories/ paolini.cfm).

The Book Report Network. "Author Profile: Christopher Paolini." Teenreads.com. Retrieved August 31, 2011 (http://www.teenreads.com/authors/au- paolini-christopher.asp#view0309).

Brown, Matthew. "Christopher Paolini: Family, Montana Landscape Shape Author." *Seattle Times*, September 22, 2008. Retrieved August 31, 2011 (http://seattletimes.nwsource.com/html/entertain- ment/2008192289_eragonauthor22.html).

"Carl Hiaasen Christopher Paolini: Carl Hiaasen on Chris Paolini Self-Published *Eragon*." YouTube. com, February 7, 2009. Retrieved August 31, 2011 (http://www.youtube.com/ watch?v=fZ734utZM4U).

"Christopher Paolini Answers Fan Questions, Part 2." YouTube.com, September 8, 2011. Retrieved September 15, 2011 (http://www.youtube.com/ watch?v=WzPKKvvL2eQ&feature=chan nel_video_title).

"Christopher Paolini—An Interview with Author." BookBrowse.com. Retrieved August 31, 2011 (http://www.bookbrowse.com/author_interviews/full/index.cfm/author_number/934/christopher-paolini).

"Christopher Paolini Interviews on Eye on Books Classic." Eyeonbooks.com, August 2005. Retrieved September 5, 2011 (http://classic.eyeonbooks.com/ibp.php?ISBN=037582670X).

"Christopher Paolini on the *Today Show*." YouTube.com, September 20, 2008. Retrieved August 31, 2011 (http://www.youtube.com/watch?v=XIE9B4fCalU).

"Christopher Paolini Unveils *Brisingr*." YouTube.com, September 20, 2008. Retrieved August 31, 2011 (http://www.youtube.com/watch?v=IbxMFys8B78).

"*Eragon* (2006)." IMDb.com. Retrieved September 5, 2011 (http://www.imdb.com/title/tt0449010/).

Goodnow, Cecelia. "*Eragon* Has Taken Teen on Fantasy Flight." Projo.com, October 20, 2008. Retrieved September 1, 2011 (http://www.projo.com/books/content/lb-wunderkind-author_10-20-08_QJBRVIO_v15.262f0c6.html).

"Guinness World Records Honors *Eragon* Author Christopher Paolini at BookExpo America." *Guinness World Records*, 2011. Retrieved September 5, 2011 (http://community.guinnessworldrecords.com/_Guinness-World-Records-Honors-Eragon-Author-Christopher-Paolini-at-BookExpo-America/blog/3706057/7691.html).

Harms, Valerie. "Teen Wizard: Chris Paolini." *Distinctly Montana*, 2007. Retrieved September 1, 2011 (http://www.distinctlymontana.com/article/teen-wizard-chris-paolini).

Haslem, Stacy. "Sharing the Power of Words." *Missoulian*, November 28, 2002. Retrieved August 31, 2011 (http://missoulian.com/article_b6adba39-a5f2-5aa3-956b-fe0613b13827.html).

Hill, Brian E., and Dee Power. *The Making of a Bestseller: Success Stories from Authors and the Editors, Agents, and Booksellers Behind Them*. Chicago, IL: Dearborn Trade Publishing, 2005.

Leonard, Tom. "Is Christopher Paolini's *Brisingr* the New Harry Potter?" *Telegraph*, September 28, 2008. Retrieved August 31, 2011 (http://www.telegraph.co.uk/culture/books/3561334/Is-Christopher-Paolinis-Brisingr-the-new-Harry-Potter.html).

Macauley, Michael, and Mark Cotta Vaz. *The Inheritance Almanac: An A-to-Z Guide to the World of Eragon*. New York, NY: Alfred A. Knopf, 2010.

Marshall, John. "Lessons in Book Promotion Pay Off for Young Self-Published Author." Seattlepi.com, January 2, 2003. Retrieved August 31, 2011 (http://www.seattlepi.com/ae/books/article/Lessons-in-book-promotion-pay-off-for-young-1104464.php).

Memmott, Carol. "Wizard of Words Writes Away." *USA TODAY*, August 30, 2005. Retrieved September 1, 2011 (http://www.usatoday.com/life/books/news/2005-08-30-paolini_x.htm).

Montana Office of Tourism. "Cool Montana Stories."
    Montanakids.com, 2007. Retrieved September 1,
    2011 (http://montanakids.com/cool_stories/).

"News About *Eragon*, Book One of the Inheritance
    Trilogy, by Christopher Paolini." Alagaesia.com, July
    12, 2005. Retrieved September 5, 2011 (http://
    www.alagaesia.com/news_moviesearch.htm).

Paolini, Talita. "Unleashing the Dragon." *Home
    Education Magazine*, March–April 2002. Retrieved
    August 31, 2011 (http://www.homeedmag.com/
    HEM/192/mapaolini.html).

"Part 1—Christopher Paolini Interviewed By Homeschool.
    com's Rebecca Kochenderfer." YouTube.com, May
    24, 2010. Retrieved September 1, 2011 (http://
    www.youtube.com/watch?v=vb5NUvsYgjg).

Peterson, Matthew. "Christopher Paolini—Online Radio
    Interview with the Author." The AuthorHour.com,
    2009. Retrieved Aug. 31, 2011 (http://theautho-
    rhour.com/christopher-paolini/).

Random House Children's Books. "*Brisingr* Release Party
    with Christopher Paolini." YouTube.com, September
    30, 2008. Retrieved September 5, 2011 (http://
    www.youtube.com/watch?v=ff_swmaCi14).

Random House, Inc. "Christopher Paolini's Inheritance
    Cycle." 2011. Retrieved August 31, 2011 (http://
    www.alagaesia.com/).

Random House, Inc. "Read the Press Release
    Announcing Inheritance First Day Sales."
    November 10, 2011. Retrieved December 1, 2011
    (http://www.alagaesia.com/news_detail.php?f=3).

Riddell, Brad. "Christopher Paolini Chats About New Book." *Boys' Life*, 2011. Retrieved August 31, 2011 (http://boyslife.org/home/5065/christpher-paolin-chats-about-new-book/).

Rider, Jane. "Young Montana Author Has Gained National Acclaim." *Missoulian*, October 12, 2003. Retrieved September 5, 2011 (http://missoulian.com/news/state-and-regional/article_21802c16-1d4c-55bc-9435-5a283c3eb8cb.html).

Roback, Diane. "'*Brisingr* Breaks Random House Children's Record." *Publishers Weekly*, September 23, 2008. Retrieved September 1, 2011 (http://www.publishersweekly.com/pw/by-topic/childrens/childrens-book-news/article/5583--brisingr--breaks-random-house-children--s-record-.html).

Shelden, Michael. "Meet the 21st-Century Tolkien." *The Telegraph*, December 22, 2003. Retrieved August 31, 2011 (http://www.telegraph.co.uk/culture/donotmigrate/3608974/Meet-the-21st-century-Tolkien.html).

Smith, Dinitia. "Finding a Middle Earth in Montana; A Teenager's Fantasy Set in a Magical Land Is a Best Seller." *New York Times*, October 7, 2003. Retrieved August 31, 2011 (http://www.nytimes.com/2003/10/07/books/07DRAG.html).

Spring, Kit. "Interview: Christopher Paolini." *Observer*, January 24, 2004. Retrieved August 31, 2011 (http://www.guardian.co.uk/books/2004/jan/25/booksforchildrenandteenagers.features).

"Transcripts—CNN Saturday Morning News." CNN.
    com, August 27, 2005. Retrieved September 1,
    2011 (http://edition.cnn.com/TRANSCRIPTS/0508/
    27/smn.03.html).

Wilcox, Ledah. "Fantasy Life." *Missoulian*, December
    16, 2002. Retrieved August 31, 2011 (http://
    missoulian.com/uncategorized/article_f660aa35-
    6674-5555-ae2f-92898d6dad39.html).

Winchester, Elizabeth. "Christopher Paolini, Author."
    Time For Kids, October 6, 2003.

Wloszczyna, Susan. "More of the 'Rings' Magic." *USA
    TODAY*, January 20, 2004. Retrieved September
    5, 2011 (http://www.usatoday.com/life/movies/
    news/2004-01-20-fantasy-films-main_x.htm).

Zipp, Yvonne. "Teen Author Wins Readers Book by
    Book." *Christian Science Monitor*, August 7,
    2003. Retrieved September 1, 2011 (http://www.
    csmonitor.com/2003/0807/p20s01-bogn.html).

ABOUT THE AUTHOR

Lisa Wade McCormick is an award-winning writer and investigative reporter. She has written fourteen nonfiction books for children. Lisa and her family live in Kansas City, Missouri. She often visits schools and libraries with her golden retriever, who is a Reading Education Assistance Dog (R.E.A.D.). The goal of the R.E.A.D. program is to improve children's literacy skills by giving them the opportunity to read to specially trained therapy dogs.

PHOTO CREDITS

Cover, pp. 3 (author portrait), 39 Newscom; cover (inset), back cover, p. 3 (inset), interior image (open book) © www.istockphoto.com/Andrzej Tokarski; cover, back cover, interior background image (pattern) (fantasy mountain), pp. 20–21 Shutterstock.com; pp. 6–7, 46–47, 54–55, 58–59 © AP Images; pp. 12–13 Doug Loneman for the New York Times/Redux; pp. 14–15 Comstock/Thinkstock; p. 16 Buyenlarge/Getty Images; p. 26 HIP/Art Resource, NY; pp. 28–29 Dave Hogan/Getty Images; p. 35 Jason Merritt/FilmMagic/Getty Images; p. 42 Chip East/Reuters/Landov; pp. 50–51 © Globe Photos/ZUMApress.com; p. 49 © Oliver Carnay/ZUMApress; pp. 62, 79 Ben Gabbe/Getty Images; pp. 64–65 John Lamparski/Getty Images; pp. 70–71 MJ Kim/Getty Images; pp. 74–75 Hector Vivas/Jam Media/LatinContent/Getty Images.

Designer: Nicole Russo; Editor: Andrea Sclarow Paskoff; Photo Researcher: Amy Feinberg